Flowers are fun to make, as well as quick and easy. Choose from five wall hangings and nine fashionable accessories. Make more flowers and leaves to decorate and embelish lots of fun projects.

LEISURE ARTS, INC.
Maumelle, Arkansas

Flowers

EASY

SHOPPING LIST

Yarn (Medium Weight)

5-Petal Flower
- [ ] Flower - 4 yards (3.5 meters)
- [ ] Contrasting Color - 12" (30.5 cm)

Billy Buttons
- [ ] Buttons - 6 yards (5.5 meters)
- [ ] Stem - 2 yards (2 meters)

Ranunculus
- [ ] 12 yards (11 meters)

Large Daisy
- [ ] White - 15 yards (13.5 meters)
- [ ] Gold - 4 yards (3.5 meters)

Small Daisy
- [ ] White - 8 yards (7.5 meters)
- [ ] Gold - 3 yards (2.5 meters)

Large Rose
- [ ] 19 yards (17.5 meters)

Small Rose
- [ ] 10 yards (9 meters)

Large Mum
- [ ] 26 yards (24 meters)

Medium Mum
- [ ] 15 yards (13.5 meters)

Small Mum
- [ ] 9 yards (8 meters)

Crochet Hook
- [ ] Size G (4 mm)
      or size indicated in project

Additional Supplies
- [ ] Yarn needle
- [ ] Polyester fiberfill for Billy Buttons & Daisy

GAUGE INFORMATION

Gauge is not of great importance; your Flowers may be a little larger or smaller without changing the overall effect.

STITCH GUIDE

TREBLE CROCHET
(abbreviated tr)
YO twice, insert hook in st indicated, YO and pull up a loop (4 loops on hook), (YO and draw through 2 loops on hook) 3 times.

SINGLE CROCHET 2 TOGETHER
(abbreviated sc2tog)
Pull up a loop in each of next 2 sc, YO and draw through all 3 loops on hook (**counts as one sc**).

5-PETAL FLOWER

Rnd 1 (Right side)**:** Make an adjustable loop to form a ring *(Figs. 1a-d, page 45)*, work 10 sc in ring; do **not** join.

Note: Loop a short piece of yarn around any stitch to mark Rnd 1 as **right** side.

Rnd 2: In each sc around work (slip st, ch 3, 2 dc, ch 3, slip st); finish off.

Using photo as a guide and Contrasting Color, embroider a straight stitch on each petal *(Fig. 4, page 46)*.

BILLY BUTTONS

BUTTON (Make 2)
Rnd 1 (Right side)**:** Make an adjustable loop to form a ring *(Figs. 1a-d, page 45)*, work 4 sc in ring; do **not** join, place marker to indicate beginning of rnd *(see Markers, page 44)*.

Note: Loop a short piece of yarn around any stitch to mark Rnd 1 as **right** side.

Rnd 2: 2 Sc in each sc around: 8 sc.

Rnd 3: Sc in each sc around.

Stuff Button with polyester fiberfill.

Rnd 4: Sc2tog around; slip st in next st, finish off leaving a long end for sewing: 4 sc.

STEMS
Ch 13.

Row 1: Slip st in second ch from hook and in next 5 chs, ch 4, slip st in second ch from hook and in last 2 chs, slip st in same ch already worked into on main ch and in last 6 chs; finish off.

With long end, sew one Button to the end of each Stem.

RANUNCULUS
BOTTOM PETALS
Rnd 1 (Right side)**:** Make an adjustable loop to form a ring *(Figs. 1a-d, page 45)*, work 6 sc in ring; do **not** join, place marker to indicate beginning of rnd *(see Markers, page 44)*.

Note: Loop a short piece of yarn around any stitch to mark Rnd 1 as **right** side.

Rnd 2: 2 Sc in each sc around: 12 sc.

Rnd 3: (Sc in next sc, 2 sc in next sc) around: 18 sc.

Rnd 4: ★ (Dc, hdc) in next sc, sc in next sc; repeat from ★ around; slip st in next dc, finish off: 27 sts.

MIDDLE PETALS
Rnds 1 and 2: Work same as Bottom Petals: 12 sc.

Rnd 3: ★ (Dc, hdc) in next sc, (sc, dc) in next sc, (hdc, sc) in next sc; repeat from ★ around; slip st in next dc, finish off: 24 sts.

TOP PETALS
Rnd 1: Work same as Bottom Petals: 6 sc.

Note: Mark Rnd 1 as **right** side.

Rnd 2: (Dc, sc) in each sc around; slip st in next dc, finish off leaving a long end for sewing: 12 sts.

Stack Petals and sew around Rnd 1, working through all 3 layers.

CENTER
Rnds 1-3: With Gold, work same as Petals: 18 sc.

Rnd 4: Sc in each sc around; slip st in next sc, finish off leaving a long end for sewing.

With long end, sew Center to Rnd 3 of Petals, stuffing with polyester fiberfill before closing.

LARGE DAISY

PETALS
Rnd 1 (Right side)**:** With White, make an adjustable loop to form a ring *(Figs. 1a-d, page 45)*, work 6 sc in ring; do **not** join, place marker to indicate beginning of rnd *(see Markers, page 44)*.

Note: Loop a short piece of yarn around any stitch to mark Rnd 1 as **right** side.

Rnd 2: 2 Sc in each sc around: 12 sc.

Rnd 3: (2 Sc in next sc, sc in next sc) around: 18 sc.

Rnd 4: ★ Ch 7; sc in second ch from hook and in next ch, hdc in next 2 chs, sc in last 2 chs, sc in next sc on Rnd 3; repeat from ★ around; slip st in first ch of first petal, finish off: 18 petals.

SMALL DAISY
PETALS
Rnd 1 (Right side)**:** With White, make an adjustable loop to form a ring *(Figs. 1a-d, page 45)*, work 6 sc in ring; do **not** join, place marker to indicate beginning of rnd *(see Markers, page 44)*.

Note: Loop a short piece of yarn around any stitch to mark Rnd 1 as **right** side.

Rnd 2: 2 Sc in each sc around: 12 sc.

Rnd 3: ★ Ch 5; sc in second ch from hook, hdc in next 2 chs, sc in last ch, sc in next sc on Rnd 2; repeat from ★ around; slip st in first ch of first petal, finish off: 12 petals.

CENTER
Rnds 1 and 2: With Gold, work same as Petals: 12 sc.

Rnd 3: Sc in each sc around; slip st in next sc, finish off leaving a long end for sewing.

With long end, sew Center to Rnd 2 of Petals, stuffing with polyester fiberfill before closing.

LARGE ROSE
Ch 21.

Row 1: 2 Dc in fourth ch from hook and in each of next 5 chs, 2 hdc in each of next 6 chs, 2 sc in each of last 6 chs: 37 sts.

Row 2: Ch 1, turn; (sc, hdc) in first sc, ★ (hdc, sc) in next st, (sc, hdc) in next st; repeat from ★ across to last dc, (hdc, sc) in last dc, leave last st unworked: 72 sts.

Row 3 (Right side)**:** Ch 1, turn; sc in first sc, 2 hdc in each of next 2 hdc, ★ sc in next 2 sc, 2 hdc in each of next 2 hdc; repeat from ★ across to last sc, sc in last sc; finish off leaving a long end for sewing: 108 sts.

With **wrong** side facing and placing the last st worked on Row 3 at the center, allow the piece to naturally curl and with long end, sew along beginning ch to hold petals in place.

SMALL ROSE
Ch 15.

Row 1: 2 Dc in fourth ch from hook and in each of next 3 chs, 2 hdc in each of next 4 chs, 2 sc in each of last 4 chs: 25 sts.

Row 2 (Right side)**:** Ch 1, turn; sc in first sc, (2 hdc in each of next 2 sts, sc in next st) across; finish off leaving a long end for sewing: 41 sts.

With **wrong** side facing and placing the first st worked on Row 2 at the center, allow the piece to naturally curl and with long end, sew along beginning ch to hold petals in place.

LARGE MUM
Ch 49.

Row 1 (Right side)**:** In second ch from hook and in each ch across work (slip st, ch 3, tr, ch 3, slip st); finish off leaving a long end for sewing.

With **wrong** side facing and placing the first st worked on Row 1 at the center, allow the piece to naturally curl and with long end, sew along beginning ch to hold petals in place.

7

MEDIUM MUM
Ch 37.

Row 1 (Right side): In second ch from hook and in each ch across work (slip st, ch 2, dc, ch 2, slip st); finish off leaving a long end for sewing.

With **wrong** side facing and placing the first st worked on Row 1 at the center, allow the piece to naturally curl and with long end, sew along beginning ch to hold petals in place.

SMALL MUM
Ch 25.

Row 1 (Right side): (Sc, dc, sc) in second ch from hook and in each ch across; finish off leaving a long end for sewing.

With **wrong** side facing and placing the first st worked on Row 1 at the center, allow the piece to naturally curl and with long end, sew along beginning ch to hold petals in place.

Leaves

 EASY

SHOPPING LIST

Yarn (Medium Weight)

Small Leaf
☐ 4 yards (3.5 meters)
Large Leaf
☐ 5 yards (4.5 meters)
Daisy Leaf
☐ 4 yards (3.5 meters)
Laurel Leaf
☐ 7 yards (6.5 meters)

Crochet Hook
☐ Size G (4 mm)
   or size needed for project

GAUGE INFORMATION

Gauge is not of great importance; your Leaves may be a little larger or smaller without changing the overall effect.

SMALL LEAF
Ch 8.

Rnd 1 (Right side)**:** 3 Dc in fourth ch from hook, dc in next ch, hdc in next ch, sc in next ch, (sc, ch 1, sc) in last ch; working in free loops of beginning ch *(Fig. 3, page 46)*, sc in next ch, hdc in next ch, dc in next ch, 3 dc in next ch; join with slip st to first st; ch 9 (stem), slip st in second ch from hook and in each ch across; finish off.

Note: Loop a short piece of yarn around any stitch to mark Rnd 1 as **right** side.

LARGE LEAF

Ch 7.

Rnd 1 (Right side)**:** 2 Sc in second ch from hook, hdc in next 3 chs, sc in next ch, 3 sc in last ch; working in free loops of beginning ch *(Fig. 3, page 46)*, sc in next ch, hdc in next 3 chs, 2 sc in next ch; join with slip st to first sc: 15 sts.

Note: Loop a short piece of yarn around any stitch to mark Rnd 1 as **right** side.

Rnd 2: Ch 1, 2 sc in same st as joining, hdc in next sc, 2 dc in each of next 2 hdc, hdc in next 2 sts, sc in next sc, (sc, ch 2, sc) in next sc, sc in next sc, hdc in next 2 sts, 2 dc in each of next 2 hdc, hdc in next sc, 2 sc in last sc; join with slip st to first sc; ch 11 (stem), slip st in second ch from hook and in each ch across; finish off.

DAISY LEAF

Ch 12.

Rnd 1 (Right side)**:** Sc in sixth ch from hook and in next ch, ch 5, (sc in next 2 chs, ch 4) twice, (sc, ch 4) twice in last ch; working in free loops of beginning ch *(Fig. 3, page 46)*, sc in next 2 chs, ch 4, (sc in next 2 chs, ch 5) twice, slip st in next ch; ch 7 (stem), slip st in second ch from hook and in each ch across; finish off.

Note: Loop a short piece of yarn around any stitch to mark Rnd 1 as **right** side.

LAUREL LEAF
TOP LEAF & STEM

Rnd 1 (Right side)**:** Ch 4, sc in second ch from hook and in next ch, 4 dc in last ch; working in free loops of beginning ch *(Fig. 3, page 46)*, sc in next 2 chs; join with slip st to first sc; ch 15 (stem), slip st in second ch from hook and in each ch across; finish off.

Note: Loop a short piece of yarn around any stitch to mark Rnd 1 as **right** side.

DOUBLE LEAVES (Make 2)
Ch 10.

Row 1 (Right side)**:** Dc in fourth ch from hook, hdc in next ch, sc in next ch, slip st in next ch, sc in next ch, hdc in next ch, (dc, ch 3, slip st) in last ch; finish off.

Note: Loop a short piece of yarn around any stitch to mark Row 1 as **right** side.

Using photo as a guide for placement, sew Double Leaves to Stem.

Antler Wall Hanging

■■□□ **EASY**

Finished Size: 4" x 12" (10 cm x 30.5 cm)

SHOPPING LIST

Yarn (Medium Weight)

- ☐ Linen - 60 yards (55 meters)
- ☐ Pink - 19 yards (17.5 meters)
- ☐ Grey - 8 yards (7.5 meters)
- ☐ Lt Blue - 8 yards (7.5 meters)
- ☐ Lt Olive - 14 yards (13 meters)
- ☐ Olive - 5 yards (4.5 meters)
- ☐ White - small amount

Crochet Hook

- ☐ Size G (4 mm)

Additional Supplies

- ☐ Yarn needle
- ☐ Strong thread (for hanger)
- ☐ Polyester fiberfill

GAUGE INFORMATION

Gauge is not of great importance; your Flowers and Leaves may be a little larger or smaller. The Antler needs a tight gauge.

STITCH GUIDE

SINGLE CROCHET 2 TOGETHER
(abbreviated sc2tog)
Pull up a loop in each of next 2 sc, YO and draw through all 3 loops on hook (**counts as one sc**).

ANTLER (Make 2)

MAIN PIECE

Rnd 1 (Right side)**:** With Linen, make an adjustable loop to form a ring *(Figs. 1a-d, page 45)*, work 4 sc in ring; do **not** join, place marker to indicate beginning of rnd *(see Markers, page 44)*.

Rnd 2: Sc in each sc around.

Rnd 3 (Increase rnd)**:** 2 Sc in next sc, sc in each sc around: 5 sc.

Rnds 4-6: Repeat Rnds 2 and 3 once, then repeat Rnd 2 once **more**: 6 sc.

Stuff piece with polyester fiberfill as you work.

Rnds 7 and 8: 2 Sc in next sc, sc in next sc, sc2tog, sc in next 2 sc.

Rnds 9 and 10: Sc in each sc around.

Rnd 11: 2 Sc in next sc, sc in each sc around: 7 sc.

Rnds 12 and 13: Sc in each sc around.

Rnd 14: 2 Sc in next sc, sc in each sc around: 8 sc.

Rnds 15-17: Sc in each sc around.

Rnds 18-20: Sc in next 2 sc, 2 sc in next sc, sc in next 3 sc, sc2tog.

Rnds 21-32: Sc in each sc around.

Rnd 33: (2 Sc in next sc, sc in next sc) around: 12 sc.

Rnd 34: Working in Back Loops Only *(Fig. 2, page 45)*, sc2tog around; slip st in next st, finish off leaving a long end for closing: 6 sc.

With long end, sew opening closed.

SHORT PIECE

Rnds 1-8: Work same as Main Piece: 6 sc.

Rnd 9: (2 Sc in next sc, sc in next sc) around; slip st in next st, finish off leaving a long end for sewing: 9 sc.

LONG PIECE

Rnds 1-6: Work same as Main Piece: 6 sc.

Stuff piece with polyester fiberfill as you work.

Rnds 7 and 8: Sc in each sc around.

Rnd 9: Sc in next 4 sc, 2 sc in next sc, sc in next sc: 7 sc.

Rnd 10: Sc in each sc around.

Rnd 11: Sc in next 4 sc, 2 sc in next sc, sc in next 2 sc: 8 sc.

Rnd 12: Sc in each sc around.

Rnd 13: Sc in next 4 sc, 2 sc in next sc, sc in next 3 sc; slip st in next st, finish off leaving a long end for sewing: 9 sc.

Using photo as a guide for placement and long ends, sew Short and Long Pieces to Main Piece.

BASE

Rnd 1 (Right side)**:** With Linen, make an adjustable loop to form a ring, work 6 sc in ring; do **not** join, place marker to indicate beginning of rnd.

Note: Loop a short piece of yarn around any stitch to mark Rnd 1 as **right** side.

Rnd 2: 2 Sc in each sc around: 12 sc.

Rnd 3: (2 Sc in next sc, sc in next sc) around: 18 sc.

Rnd 4: (2 Sc in next sc, sc in next 2 sc) around: 24 sc.

Rnd 5: (2 Sc in next sc, sc in next 3 sc) around: 30 sc.

Rnd 6: (2 Sc in next sc, sc in next 4 sc) around; slip st in next sc, finish off leaving a long end for sewing: 36 sc.

Sew both Antlers to Base.

FLOWERS & LEAVES

• With Lt Blue, make two 5-Petal Flowers, page 3, working straight sts with White.
• With Pink, make Large Rose, page 6.
• With Grey, make 2 Small Leaves, page 9.
• With Olive, make Large Leaf, page 10.
• With Lt Olive, make 2 Laurel Leaves, page 11.

Using photo as a guide for placement, sew Leaves to Base, then sew one 5-Petal Flower on each side and Large Rose at center.

Using a 10" (25.5 cm) piece of strong thread, sew ends at back of Antlers for hanger.

Wreath

■■□□ EASY

Finished Size: 14" (35.5 cm) diameter wreath

SHOPPING LIST

Yarn (Medium Weight)

- ☐ Linen - 55 yards (50.5 meters)
- ☐ Lt Olive - 42 yards (38.5 meters)
- ☐ Pink - 38 yards (34.5 meters)
- ☐ Ecru - 28 yards (25.5 meters)
- ☐ Rose - 26 yards (24 meters)
- ☐ Gold - 18 yards (16.5 meters)
- ☐ White - 18 yards (16.5 meters)
- ☐ Lt Blue - 16 yards (14.5 meters)
- ☐ Green - 18 yards (16.5 meters)
- ☐ Lt Green - 14 yards (13 meters)
- ☐ Olive - 10 yards (9 meters)

Crochet Hook

- ☐ Size G (4 mm)

Additional Supplies

- ☐ Yarn needle
- ☐ 14" (35.5 cm) Grapevine wreath
- ☐ Polyester fiberfill

GAUGE INFORMATION

Gauge is not of great importance; your Flowers and Leaves may be a little larger or smaller. The Antler needs a tight gauge.

STITCH GUIDE

SINGLE CROCHET 2 TOGETHER
(abbreviated sc2tog)

Pull up a loop in each of next 2 sc, YO and draw through all 3 loops on hook (**counts as one sc**).

ANTLER (Make 2)

MAIN PIECE

Rnd 1 (Right side)**:** With Linen, make an adjustable loop to form a ring *(Figs. 1a-d, page 45)*, work 4 sc in ring; do **not** join, place marker to indicate beginning of rnd *(see Markers, page 44)*.

Rnd 2: Sc in each sc around.

Rnd 3 (Increase rnd)**:** 2 Sc in next sc, sc in each sc around: 5 sc.

Rnds 4-6: Repeat Rnds 2 and 3 once, then repeat Rnd 2 once **more**: 6 sc.

Stuff piece with polyester fiberfill as you work.

Rnds 7 and 8: 2 Sc in next sc, sc in next sc, sc2tog, sc in next 2 sc.

Rnds 9 and 10: Sc in each sc around.

Rnd 11: 2 Sc in next sc, sc in each sc around: 7 sc.

Rnds 12 and 13: Sc in each sc around.

Rnd 14: 2 Sc in next sc, sc in each sc around: 8 sc.

Rnds 15-17: Sc in each sc around.

Rnds 18-20: Sc in next 2 sc, 2 sc in next sc, sc in next 3 sc, sc2tog.

Rnds 21-32: Sc in each sc around.

Rnd 33: (2 Sc in next sc, sc in next sc) around: 12 sc.

Rnd 34: Working in Back Loops Only *(Fig. 2, page 45)*, sc2tog around; slip st in next st, finish off leaving a long end for closing: 6 sc.

With long end, sew opening closed.

SHORT PIECE

Rnds 1-8: Work same as Main Piece: 6 sc.

Rnd 9: (2 Sc in next sc, sc in next sc) around; slip st in next st, finish off leaving a long end for sewing: 9 sc.

LONG PIECE

Rnds 1-6: Work same as Main Piece: 6 sc.

Stuff piece with polyester fiberfill as you work.

Rnds 7 and 8: Sc in each sc around.

Rnd 9: Sc in next 4 sc, 2 sc in next sc, sc in next sc: 7 sc.

Rnd 10: Sc in each sc around.

Rnd 11: Sc in next 4 sc, 2 sc in next sc, sc in next 2 sc: 8 sc.

Rnd 12: Sc in each sc around.

Rnd 13: Sc in next 4 sc, 2 sc in next sc, sc in next 3 sc; slip st in next st, finish off leaving a long end for sewing: 9 sc.

Using photo as a guide for placement and long ends, sew Short and Long Pieces to Main Piece. Sew both Antlers to wreath.

HANGER

With Ecru, ch 31.

Row 1: Sc in second ch from hook and in each ch across; finish off.

FLOWERS & LEAVES

• With Lt Blue, make four 5-Petal Flowers, page 3, working straight sts with White.
• With Gold for Buttons and Lt Green for Stems, make 2 Billy Buttons, page 3.
• With Ecru, make two Ranunculus, page 4.
• Make two Small Daisies, page 5.
• With Pink, make two Large Roses, page 6.
• With Rose, make one Large Mum, page 7.
• With Green, make two Small Leaves, page 9.
• Make six Large Leaves, page 10, two **each** using Lt Green, Green, and Olive.
• With Lt Olive, make six Laurel Leaves, page 11.

Using photo, page 17, as a guide for placement, sew Flowers and Leaves to wreath.

Sew Hanger to back of wreath.

Garland

◖◼◻◻◗ **EASY**

Finished Size: 4½ feet (137 cm) long

SHOPPING LIST

Yarn (Medium Weight) 🧶4
- ☐ Rose - 135 yards (123 meters)
- ☐ Off White - 75 yards (68.5 meters)
- ☐ Green - 60 yards (55 meters)

Crochet Hook
- ☐ Size G (4 mm)

Additional Supplies
- ☐ Yarn needle

GAUGE INFORMATION

Gauge is not of great importance; your Flowers and Leaves may be a little larger or smaller without changing the overall effect.

GARLAND

First End Leaf (Right side): With Green, ch 4, sc in second ch from hook and in next ch, 4 dc in last ch; working in free loops of beginning ch *(Fig. 3, page 46)*, sc in next 2 chs; join with slip st to first sc: 8 sts.

Note: Loop a short piece of yarn around any stitch to mark Leaf as **right** side.

Chain: Ch 251; sc in second ch from hook and in each ch across; finish off.

Second End Leaf: Work same as First End Leaf; finish off leaving a long end for sewing.

With long end, sew Leaf to second end of long chain.

FLOWERS & LEAVES

• With Off White, make six Ranunculus, page 4.
• With Rose, make seven Large Roses, page 6.
• With Green, make sixteen Double Leaves, page 11.

Using photo as a guide for placement, sew Flowers and Leaves to chain.

Burlap & Flowers

■■□□ EASY

Finished Size: 8" (20.5 cm) diameter ring

SHOPPING LIST

Yarn (Medium Weight)

- ☐ Lt Gold - 26 yards (24 meters)
- ☐ Off White - 25 yards (23 meters)
- ☐ Green - 19 yards (17.5 meters)
- ☐ Dk Green - 18 yards (16.5 meters)
- ☐ Rose - 8 yards (7.5 meters)

Crochet Hook

- ☐ Size G (4 mm)

Additional Supplies

- ☐ Yarn needle
- ☐ 8" (20.5 cm) Embroidery hoop
- ☐ Burlap - 10" (25.5 cm) square
- ☐ Fabric glue

GAUGE INFORMATION

Gauge is not of great importance; your Flowers and Leaves may be a little larger or smaller without changing the overall effect.

FLOWERS & LEAVES

- With Rose, make two 5-Petal Flowers, page 3, working straight sts with Off White.
- With Off White, make two Ranunculus, page 4.
- With Lt Gold, make one Large Mum, page 7.
- With Dk Green, make two Small Leaves, page 9.
- With Dk Green, make two Large Leaves, page 10.
- With Green, make one Large Leaf, page 10.
- With Green, make two Laurel Leaves, page 11.

Place the burlap inside the hoop, being sure to make it taut in the hoop. On the back, trim the burlap to ½" (12 mm) around. Glue the burlap to the inside of the hoop.

Using photo as a guide for placement, sew Flowers and Leaves to burlap.

Dream Catcher

EASY

Finished Size: 8" (20.5 cm) diameter ring

SHOPPING LIST

Yarn (Medium Weight) MEDIUM 4

- ☐ White - 25 yards (23 meters)
- ☐ Lt Grey - 20 yards (18.5 meters)
- ☐ Pink - 20 yards (18.5 meters)
- ☐ Lt Rose - 19 yards (17.5 meters)
- ☐ Taupe - 18 yards (16.5 meters)
- ☐ Lt Olive - 14 yards (13 meters)
- ☐ Olive - 5 yards (4.5 meters)

Crochet Hook

- ☐ Size G (4 mm) **or** size needed for gauge

Additional Supplies

- ☐ Yarn needle
- ☐ 8" (20.5 cm) Embroidery hoop
- ☐ Strong white thread
- ☐ Straight pins

GAUGE INFORMATION

Gauge Swatch: 2½" (6.25 cm) diameter at points

Work same as Doily through Rnd 2.

DOILY

Rnd 1 (Right side): With White, ch 6, sc in first ch made, (ch 5, sc in same ch) 4 times, ch 3, hdc in same ch to form last ch-5 sp: 6 ch-5 sps.

Note: Loop a short piece of yarn around any stitch to mark Rnd 1 as **right** side.

Rnd 2: Ch 1, sc in last sp made, ch 5, (sc in next ch-5 sp, ch 5) around; join with slip st to first sc.

Rnd 3: Ch 1, sc in same st as joining, ch 5, sc in next ch-5 sp, ★ ch 5, sc in next sc, ch 5, sc in next ch-5 sp; repeat from ★ around, ch 3, hdc in first sc to form last ch-5 sp: 12 ch-5 sps.

Rnd 4: Ch 1, sc in last sp made, (ch 5, sc in next ch-5 sp) around, ch 3, hdc in first sc to form last ch-5 sp.

Rnd 5: Ch 1, sc in last sp made, ch 6, (sc in next ch-5 sp, ch 6) around; join with slip st to first sc.

Rnd 6: Ch 1, in each ch-6 sp around work (2 sc, hdc, dc, ch 2, dc, hdc, 2 sc); join with slip st to first sc, finish off.

Wind Taupe around the inside piece of the embroidery hoop, covering the entire piece; using yarn needle, secure yarn ends.

Place Doily inside hoop and pin the ch-2 sps on Rnd 6 to the hoop, evenly spaced around; then sew points in place with strong thread. Attach White for hanger.

FLOWERS & LEAVES
• With Lt Rose, make one Large Rose, page 6.
• With Pink, make 2 Small Roses, page 7.
• With Taupe, make 2 Small Leaves, page 9.
• With Olive, make one Large Leaf, page 10.
• With Lt Olive, make 2 Laurel Leaves, page 11.

Using photo as a guide for placement, sew Flowers and Leaves to ring.

FRINGE
Cut 30 strands of Lt Grey, each 22" (56 cm) long. Using photo as a guide for placement and holding 3 strands together, add 10 fringes around hoop *(Figs. 5a & b, page 46)*.

Barrettes

■■□□ **EASY**

Finished Size: Approximately 4" (10 cm) diameter

SHOPPING LIST
Yarn (Medium Weight) 🧶4
Daisy
- ☐ Green - 16 yards (14.5 meters)
- ☐ Gold - 9 yards (8 meters)
- ☐ White - 8 yards (7.5 meters)
- ☐ Lt Green - 6 yards (5.5 meters)

Flower Bouquet
- ☐ Pink - 19 yards (17.5 meters)
- ☐ Lt Olive - 14 yards (13 meters)
- ☐ Ecru - 10 yards (9 meters)
- ☐ Lt Blue - 8 yards (7.5 meters)
- ☐ Olive - 4 yards (3.5 meters)
- ☐ White - small amount

Mum
- ☐ Rose - 26 yards (24 meters)
- ☐ Lt Olive - 14 yards (13 meters)
- ☐ Olive - 5 yards (4.5 meters)

Crochet Hook
- ☐ Size G (4 mm)

Additional Supplies
- ☐ Yarn needle
- ☐ Polyester fiberfill (for Daisy Barrette)
- ☐ Barrette or clip

GAUGE INFORMATION
Gauge is not of great importance; your Flowers and Leaves may be a little larger or smaller without changing the overall effect.

Daisy

Flower
Bouquet

Mum

BASE

Rnd 1 (Right side)**:** With Green or Lt Olive, make an adjustable loop to form a ring *(Figs. 1a-d, page 45)*, work 6 sc in ring; do **not** join, place marker to indicate beginning of rnd *(see Markers, page 44)*.

Note: Loop a short piece of yarn around any stitch to mark Rnd 1 as **right** side.

Rnd 2: 2 Sc in each sc around: 12 sc.

Rnd 3: (2 Sc in next sc, sc in next sc) around: 18 sc.

Rnd 4: (2 Sc in next sc, sc in next 2 sc) around: 24 sc.

Rnd 5: (2 Sc in next sc, sc in next 3 sc) around; slip st in next sc, finish off: 30 sc.

Sew barrette or clip to **right** side of Base.

DAISY

• With Gold for Buttons and Lt Green for Stems, make one Billy Buttons, page 3.
• Make one Small Daisy, page 5.
• With Lt Green, make one Small Leaf, page 9.
• With Green, make one Large Leaf, page 10.
• With Green, make one Daisy Leaf, page 10.

Using photo as a guide for placement, sew Flowers and Leaves to Base.

FLOWER BOUQUET

- With Lt Blue, make two 5-Petal Flowers, page 3, working straight sts with White.
- With Pink, make one Large Rose, page 6.
- With Ecru, make one Small Rose, page 7.
- With Olive, make one Small Leaf, page 9.
- With Lt Olive, make one Laurel Leaf, page 11.

Using photo as a guide for placement, sew Flowers and Leaves to Base.

MUM

- With Rose, make one Large Mum, page 7.
- With Olive, make one Large Leaf, page 10.
- With Lt Olive, make one Laurel Leaf, page 11.

Using photo as a guide for placement, sew Flower and Leaves to Base.

Floral Cowl

■■□□ EASY

Finished Size: 25¾" circumference x 10" wide before folding
(65.5 cm x 25.5 cm)

SHOPPING LIST

Yarn (Medium Weight) 🧶4

[3 ounces, 197 yards
(85 grams, 180 meters) per skein]:

☐ Main Color - 1 skein
☐ Contrasting Color - 70 yards
(64 meters)

Crochet Hook

☐ Size I (5.5 mm)
or size needed for gauge

Additional Supplies

☐ Yarn needle

GAUGE INFORMATION

In pattern,
14 sts and 10 rows = 3¾"
(9.5 cm)

Gauge Swatch: 4" (10 cm)
square
With Main Color, ch 16.

Row 1: Hdc in second ch from
hook, ★ ch 1, skip next ch, hdc in
next ch; repeat from ★ across:
15 sts.

Row 2: Ch 1, turn; hdc in first hdc
and in next ch-1 sp, (ch 1, hdc in
next ch-1 sp) across, hdc in last
hdc.

Row 3: Ch 1, turn; hdc in first hdc,
ch 1, (hdc in next ch-1 sp, ch 1)
across, skip next hdc, hdc in last
hdc.

Rows 4-10: Repeat Rows 2 and 3,
3 times; then repeat Row 2 once
more.
Finish off.

COWL

With Main Color, ch 96; being careful **not** to twist ch, join with slip st to form a ring.

Rnd 1: Ch 1, hdc in each ch around; join with slip st to first hdc: 96 hdc.

Rnd 2 (Right side)**:** Ch 1, turn; hdc in same st as joining, ch 1, skip next hdc, ★ hdc in next hdc, ch 1, skip next hdc; repeat from ★ around; join with slip st to first hdc: 48 hdc and 48 ch-1 sps.

Note: Loop a short piece of yarn around any stitch to mark Rnd 2 as **right** side.

Rnds 3-23: Ch 1, turn; (hdc in next ch-1 sp, ch 1) around; join with slip st to first hdc.

Rnd 24: Ch 1, turn; 2 hdc in each ch-1 sp around; join with slip st to first hdc, finish off: 96 hdc.

Rnd 25: With **wrong** side facing, join Contrasting Color with sc in same st as joining *(see Joining With Sc, page 44)*; ch 2, skip next 2 hdc, ★ sc in next hdc, ch 2, skip next 2 hdc; repeat from ★ around; join with slip st to first sc: 32 sc and 32 ch-2 sps.

Rnd 26: Ch 1, turn; (sc, ch 2) twice in each ch-2 sp around; join with slip st to first sc: 64 sc and 64 ch-2 sps.

Rnd 27: Turn; slip st in first ch-2 sp, (sc, hdc, sc) in next ch-2 sp, ★ slip st in next ch-2 sp, (sc, hdc, sc) in next ch-2 sp; repeat from ★ around; join with slip st to first slip st, finish off.

Fold top 12 rows to **right** side.

FLOWERS & LEAF

With Contrasting Color, make:
* Ranunculus, page 4.
* Small Rose, page 7.
* One Small Leaf, page 9.

Using photo as a guide for placement, sew Flowers and Leaf to Cowl.

With Main Color, embroider French knot in center of Ranunculus *(Fig. A)*.

FRENCH KNOT

Bring needle up at 1. Wrap yarn around the needle and insert needle at 2, holding end of yarn with non-stitching fingers *(Fig. A)*. Tighten knot; then pull needle through, holding yarn until it must be released.

Fig. A

Daisy Purse

◼◼◻◻ **EASY**

Finished Size: 10" wide x 12" high (25.5 cm x 30.5 cm)

SHOPPING LIST

Yarn (Medium Weight) 🧶 4

[3.5 ounces, 170 yards
(100 grams, 156 meters) per skein]:
- ☐ Main Color - 2 skeins
- ☐ White - 23 yards (21 meters)
- ☐ Gold - 13 yards (12 meters)
- ☐ Lt Green - 10 yards (9 meters)

Crochet Hooks
- ☐ Size G (4 mm) **and**
- ☐ Size I (5.5 mm)
  or sizes needed for gauge

Additional Supplies
- ☐ Yarn needle
- ☐ Polyester fiberfill

GAUGE INFORMATION

With larger size hook,
   12 hdc = 4" (10 cm);
   10 rows = 4¼" (10.75 cm)

Gauge Swatch: 4" wide x 4¼" high
   (10 cm x 10.75 cm)
With larger size hook and Main
Color, ch 14.
Work same as Back for 10 rows;
finish off: 12 hdc.

BACK

With larger size hook and Main Color, ch 32.

Row 1 (Right side)**:** Hdc in third ch from hook and in each ch across: 30 hdc.

Note: Loop a short piece of yarn around any stitch to mark Row 1 as **right** side.

Rows 2-28: Ch 2 **(does not count as a st)**, turn; hdc in each hdc across.

Finish off.

FRONT

Work same as Back; do **not** finish off.

Joining: Holding pieces with **wrong** sides together and working through **both** pieces, sc evenly across end of rows; working in free loops of beginning chs *(Fig. 3, page 46)*, 3 sc in first ch, sc in each ch across to last ch, 3 sc in last ch; sc evenly across end of rows; slip st in next st, finish off.

SHOULDER STRAP

With larger size hook and Main Color, ch 142.

Rows 1 and 2: Work same as Back: 140 hdc.

Finish off leaving a long end for sewing.

Sew Strap to top edge of Front and Back at sides.

FRINGE

Cut 42 strands of Main Color, each 15" (38 cm) long. Holding 6 strands together, add fringe at bottom corners and 5 more evenly spaced across *(Figs. 5a & b, page 46)*.

FLOWERS & LEAF

Use smaller size hook for all Flowers and Leaves.

• With Gold for Buttons and Lt Green for Stems, make one Billy Buttons, page 3.
• Make one Large Daisy, page 5.
• Make one Small Daisy, page 5.
• With Lt Green, make two Daisy Leaves, page 10.

Using photo as a guide for placement, sew Flowers and Leaves to Front.

Drawstring Purse

■■□□ **EASY**

Finished Size: 2½" diameter at bottom x 6" high (6.5 cm x 15 cm)

SHOPPING LIST

Yarn (Medium Weight)

- ☐ Green - 70 yards (64 meters)
- ☐ Taupe - 60 yards (55 meters)
- ☐ Rose - 30 yards (27.5 meters)
- ☐ White - 25 yards (23 meters)
- ☐ Aqua - 12 yards (11 meters)
- ☐ Yellow - 9 yards (8 meters)

Crochet Hook

- ☐ Size G (4 mm)
  or size needed for gauge

Additional Supplies

- ☐ Yarn needle
- ☐ Polyester fiberfill

GAUGE INFORMATION

Gauge Swatch: 2½" (6.5 cm)
  diameter
Work same as Bottom.

BOTTOM

Rnd 1 (Right side)**:** With Taupe, make an adjustable loop to form a ring *(Figs. 1a-d, page 45)*, work 6 sc in ring; do **not** join, place marker to indicate beginning of rnd *(see Markers, page 44)*.

Note: Loop a short piece of yarn around any stitch to mark Rnd 1 as **right** side.

Rnd 2: 2 Sc in each sc around: 12 sc.

Rnd 3: (2 Sc in next sc, sc in next sc) around: 18 sc.

Rnd 4: (2 Sc in next sc, sc in next 2 sc) around: 24 sc.

Rnd 5: (2 Sc in next sc, sc in next 3 sc) around: 30 sc.

Rnd 6: (2 Sc in next sc, sc in next 4 sc) around: 36 sc.

SIDES

Rnd 1: Working in Back Loops Only *(Fig. 2, page 45)*, sc in each sc around.

Rnd 2: Working in both loops, (2 sc in next sc, sc in next 11 sc) around: 39 sc.

Rnd 3: Sc in each sc around.

Rnd 4: (2 Sc in next sc, sc in next 12 sc) around: 42 sc.

Rnd 5: Sc in each sc around.

Rnd 6: (2 Sc in next sc, sc in next 13 sc) around: 45 sc.

Rnd 7: Sc in each sc around.

Rnd 8: (2 Sc in next sc, sc in next 14 sc) around: 48 sc.

Rnd 9: Sc in each sc around.

Rnd 10: Working in Front Loops Only, (2 sc in next sc, sc in next 7 sc) around; slip st in next sc, finish off: 54 sc.

Rnd 11: With **right** side facing and working in free loops only of Rnd 9 *(Fig. A)*, join Green with slip st in same st as joining; sc in same st and in each sc around, place marker to indicate beginning of rnd: 48 sc.

Fig. A

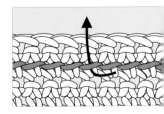

Rnd 12: (2 Hdc in next sc, hdc in next 7 sc) around: 54 hdc.

Rnds 13-21: Hdc in each hdc around.

Rnd 22 (Eyelet rnd)**:** Hdc in next 3 hdc, ch 1, skip next hdc, (hdc in next 5 hdc, ch 1, skip next hdc) 8 times, sc in next 2 hdc; slip st in next hdc, finish off: 50 hdc and 10 ch-1 sps.

DRAWSTRING

With Green, ch 80; finish off.

Weave Drawstring through ch-1 sps on Eyelet rnd; tie ends together and trim to 1" (2.5 cm).

FLOWERS

• With Aqua, make three 5-Petal Flowers, page 3, working straight sts with White.
• Make three Small Daisies, page 5, working Centers with Yellow.
• With Rose, make three Small Roses, page 7.

Sew Flowers to Sides of purse as desired.

Headbands

◼◼◻◻ **EASY**

Finished Size: Band is approximately 12" (30.5 cm) long

SHOPPING LIST

Yarn (Medium Weight)

Wildflowers
- ☐ Band (Brown) - 16 yards (14.5 meters)
- ☐ White - 16 yards (14.5 meters)
- ☐ Pink - 12 yards (11 meters)
- ☐ Green - 8 yards (7.5 meters)
- ☐ Lt Blue - 8 yards (7.5 meters)
- ☐ Gold - 6 yards (5.5 meters)
- ☐ Lt Green - 4 yards (3.5 meters)

Ranunculus
- ☐ Band (Brown) - 16 yards (14.5 meters)
- ☐ Ecru - 12 yards (11 meters)
- ☐ Green - 4 yards (3.5 meters)

Rose
- ☐ Pink - 19 yards (17.5 meters)
- ☐ Band (Lt Grey) - 16 yards (14.5 meters)
- ☐ Ecru - 12 yards (11 meters)
- ☐ Olive - 9 yards (8 meters)
- ☐ Lt Olive - 7 yards (6.5 meters)

Crochet Hook
- ☐ Size G (4 mm)

Additional Supplies
- ☐ Yarn needle
- ☐ Polyester fiberfill (for Wildflowers Headband)

GAUGE INFORMATION

Gauge is not of great importance; your Flowers and Leaves may be a little larger or smaller without changing the overall effect.

Wildflowers

Ranunculus

Rose

41

BAND

With Band color, ch 42.

Row 1: 2 Hdc in third ch from hook, hdc in each ch across to last ch, 4 hdc in last ch; working in free loops of beginning ch *(Fig. 3, page 46)*, hdc in next 38 chs, 2 hdc in next ch, slip st in next ch, ch 70; finish off.

Join Band color with slip st at opposite end; ch 70, finish off.

WILDFLOWERS

Using Lt Blue, make two 5-Petal Flowers, page 3, working straight sts with White.
Using Pink, make one Ranunculus, page 4.
Make two Small Daisies, page 5.
Using Green, make two Small Leaves, page 9.
Using Lt Green, make one Small Leaf, page 9.

Using photo as a guide for placement, sew Flowers and Leaves to Band.

RANUNCULUS

Using Ecru, make one Ranunculus, page 4.
Using Green, make one Small Leaf, page 9.

Using photo as a guide for placement, sew Flower and Leaf to Band.

ROSE

• With Ecru, make one Ranunculus, page 4.
• With Pink, make one Large Rose, page 6.
• With Olive, make one Small Leaf, page 9.
• With Olive, make one Large Leaf, page 10.
• With Lt Olive, make one Laurel Leaf, page 11.

Using photo as a guide for placement, sew Flowers and Leaves to Band.

General Instructions

ABBREVIATIONS

ch(s)	chain(s)
cm	centimeters
dc	double crochet(s)
hdc	half double crochet(s)
mm	millimeters
Rnd(s)	Round(s)
sc	single crochet(s)
sc2tog	single crochet 2 together
sp(s)	space(s)
st(s)	stitch(es)
tr	treble crochet(s)
YO	yarn over

SYMBOLS & TERMS

★ — work instructions following ★ as many **more** times as indicated in addition to the first time.

( ) or [ ] — work enclosed instructions **as many** times as specified by the number immediately following **or** work all enclosed instructions in the stitch or space indicated **or** contains explanatory remarks.

colon (:) — the number(s) given after a colon at the end of a row or round denote(s) the number of stitches or spaces you should have on that row or round.

Yarn Weight Symbol & Names	LACE 0	SUPER FINE 1	FINE 2	LIGHT 3	MEDIUM 4	BULKY 5	SUPER BULKY 6	JUMBO 7
Type of Yarns in Category	Fingering, size 10 crochet thread	Sock, Fingering, Baby	Sport, Baby	DK, Light Worsted	Worsted, Afghan, Aran	Chunky, Craft, Rug	Super Bulky, Roving	Jumbo, Roving
Crochet Gauge* Ranges in Single Crochet to 4" (10 cm)	32-42 sts**	21-32 sts	16-20 sts	12-17 sts	11-14 sts	8-11 sts	6-9 sts	5 sts and fewer
Advised Hook Size Range	Steel*** 6 to 8, Regular hook B-1	B-1 to E-4	E-4 to 7	7 to I-9	I-9 to K-10½	K-10½ to M/N-13	M/N-13 to Q	Q and larger

*GUIDELINES ONLY: The chart above reflects the most commonly used gauges and hook sizes for specific yarn categories.

** Lace weight yarns are usually crocheted with larger hooks to create lacy openwork patterns. Accordingly, a gauge range is difficult to determine. Always follow the gauge stated in your pattern.

*** Steel crochet hooks are sized differently from regular hooks–the higher the number, the smaller the hook, which is the reverse of regular hook sizing.

GAUGE

Exact gauge is **essential** for proper size. Before beginning your project, make the sample swatch given in the individual instructions in the yarn and hook specified. After completing the swatch, measure it, counting your stitches and rows carefully. If your swatch is larger or smaller than specified, **make another, changing hook size to get the correct gauge**. Keep trying until you find the size hook that will give you the specified gauge.

MARKERS

Markers are used to help distinguish the beginning of each round being worked. Place a 2" (5 cm) scrap piece of yarn before the first stitch of each round, moving the marker after each round is complete.

JOINING WITH SC

When instructed to join with sc, begin with a slip knot on hook. Insert hook in stitch or space indicated, YO and pull up a loop, YO and draw through both loops on hook.

CROCHET TERMINOLOGY	
UNITED STATES	INTERNATIONAL
slip stitch (slip st) =	single crochet (sc)
single crochet (sc) =	double crochet (dc)
half double crochet (hdc) =	half treble crochet (htr)
double crochet (dc) =	treble crochet (tr)
treble crochet (tr) =	double treble crochet (dtr)
double treble crochet (dtr) =	triple treble crochet (ttr)
triple treble crochet (tr tr) =	quadruple treble crochet (qtr)
skip =	miss

CROCHET HOOKS																	
U.S.	B-1	C-2	D-3	E-4	F-5	G-6	7	H-8	I-9	J-10	K-10½	L-11	M/N-13	N/P-15	P/Q	Q	S
Metric - mm	2.25	2.75	3.25	3.5	3.75	4	4.5	5	5.5	6	6.5	8	9	10	15	16	19

■□□□ BEGINNER	Projects for first-time crocheters using basic stitches. Minimal shaping.
■■□□ EASY	Projects using yarn with basic stitches, repetitive stitch patterns, simple color changes, and simple shaping and finishing.
■■■□ INTERMEDIATE	Projects using a variety of techniques, such as basic lace patterns or color patterns, mid-level shaping and finishing.
■■■■ EXPERIENCED	Projects with intricate stitch patterns, techniques and dimension, such as non-repeating patterns, multi-color techniques, fine threads, small hooks, detailed shaping and refined finishing.

ADJUSTABLE LOOP

Wind yarn around two fingers to form a ring *(Fig. 1a)*. Slide yarn off fingers and grasp the strands at the top of the ring *(Fig. 1b)*. Insert hook from **front** to **back** into the ring, pull up a loop, YO and draw through loop on hook to lock ring *(Fig. 1c)* (st made does **not** count as part of beginning ch). Working around both strands, follow instructions to work sts in the ring, then pull yarn tail to close *(Fig. 1d)*.

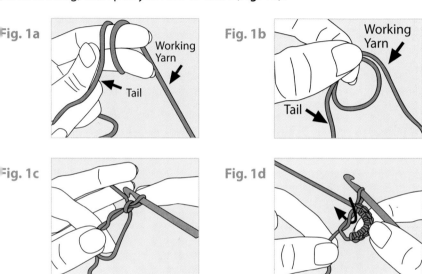

Fig. 1a — Working Yarn, Tail

Fig. 1b — Working Yarn, Tail

Fig. 1c

Fig. 1d

BACK OR FRONT LOOPS ONLY

Work only in loop(s) indicated by arrow *(Fig. 2)*.

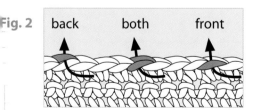

Fig. 2 — back   both   front

FREE LOOPS OF A CHAIN

When instructed to work in free loops of a chain, work in loop indicated by arrow *(Fig. 3)*.

Fig. 3

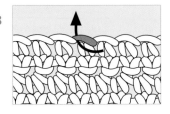

STRAIGHT STITCH

Straight stitch is just what the name implies, a single, straight stitch. Come up at 1 and go down at 2 *(Fig. 4)*.

Fig. 4

FRINGE

Cut a piece of cardboard 5" (12.5 cm) wide and half as long as length of strands indicated in individual instructions. Wind the yarn loosely and evenly around the cardboard as many times as strands needed, then cut across one end.

Hold together as many strands as specified in individual instructions; fold in half.

With **wrong** side facing and using a crochet hook, draw the folded end up through a stitch or space and pull the loose ends through the folded end *(Fig. 5a)*; draw the knot up tightly *(Fig. 5b)*. Repeat, spacing as specified in individual instructions. Lay piece on a hard surface and trim the ends.

Fig. 5a

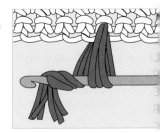

Fig. 5b

Yarn Information

The items in this book were made using Medium Weight yarn. Any brand of Medium Weight yarn may be used. It is best to refer to the yardage/meters when determining how many balls or skeins to purchase. Remember, to arrive at the finished size, it is the GAUGE/TENSION that is important, not the brand of yarn.

For your convenience, listed below are the specific yarns used to create our photography models. Because yarn manufacturers make frequent changes in their product lines, you may sometimes find it necessary to use a substitute yarn or to search for the discontinued product at alternate suppliers (locally or online).

ANTLER WALL HANGING
Lion Brand® Vanna's Choice®
Linen - #099 Linen
Pink - #101 Pink
Grey - #149 Silver Grey
Lt Blue - #105 Silver Blue
Lt Olive - #173 Dusty Green
Olive - #174 Olive
White - #100 White

WREATH
Lion Brand® Vanna's Choice®
Linen - #099 Linen
Lt Olive - #173 Dusty Green
Pink - #101 Pink
Ecru - #098 Fisherman
Rose - #142 Rose
Gold - #158 Mustard
White - #100 White
Lt Blue - #105 Silver Blue
Green - #172 Kelly Green
Lt Green - #171 Fern
Olive - #174 Olive

GARLAND
Red Heart® Soft
Rose - #9770 Rose Blush
Off White - #4601 Off White
Green - #9522 Leaf

BURLAP & FLOWERS
Red Heart® Soft
Lt Gold - #9114 Honey
Off White - #4601 Off White
Green - #9522 Leaf
Dk Green - #9523 Dk Leaf
Rose - #9770 Rose Blush

DREAM CATCHER
Lion Brand® Vanna's Choice®
White - #100 White
Lt Grey - #150 Pale Grey
Pink - #101 Pink
Lt Rose - #140 Dusty Rose
Taupe - #125 Taupe
Lt Olive - #173 Dusty Green
Olive - #174 Olive

BARRETTES

Lion Brand® Vanna's Choice®

Daisy

Green - #172 Kelly Green
Gold - #158 Mustard
White - #100 White
Lt Green - #171 Fern

Flower Bouquet

Pink - #101 Pink
Lt Olive - #173 Dusty Green
Ecru - #098 Fisherman
Lt Blue - #105 Silver Blue
Olive - #174 Olive
White - #100 White

Mum

Rose - #142 Rose
Lt Olive - #173 Dusty Green
Olive - #174 Olive

FLORAL COWL

Lion Brand® Wool-Ease®

Main Color - #403 Mushroom
Contrasting Color - #099 Fisherman

DAISY PURSE

Lion Brand® Vanna's Choice®

Main Color - #099 Linen
White - #100 White
Gold - #158 Mustard
Lt Green - #171 Fern

DRAWSTRING PURSE

Red Heart® Soft

Green - #9522 Leaf
Taupe - #9274 Biscuit
Rose - #9770 Rose Blush
White - #4600 White
Aqua - #9520 Seafoam
Yellow - #4616 Lemon

HEADBANDS

Lion Brand® Vanna's Choice®

Wildflowers

Brown - #403 Barley
White - #100 White
Pink - #101 Pink
Green - #172 Kelly Green
Lt Blue - #105 Silver Blue
Gold - #158 Mustard
Lt Green - #171 Fern

Ranunculus

Brown - #403 Barley
Ecru - #098 Fisherman
Green - #172 Kelly Green

Rose

Pink - #101 Pink
Lt Grey - #150 Pale Grey
Ecru - #098 Fisherman
Olive - #174 Olive
Lt Olive - #173 Dusty Green

Production Team: Instructional/Technical Writer - Cathy Hardy; Senior Graphic Artist - Lora Puls; Graphic Artist - Kellie McAnulty; Photo Stylist - Lori Wenger; and Photographer - Jason Masters.